AQA (B) GCSE
Religious Studies

GCSE Revision GUIDE

Unit 2

Religion and Life Issues

Sheila Butler

Philip Allan, an imprint of Hodder Education, an Hachette UK company, Blenheim Court, George Street, Banbury, Oxfordshire OX16 5BH

Orders
Bookpoint Ltd, 130 Milton Park, Abingdon, Oxfordshire OX14 4SB
tel: 01235 827827
fax: 01235 400401
e-mail: education@bookpoint.co.uk
Lines are open 9.00 a.m.–5.00 p.m., Monday to Saturday, with a 24-hour message answering service. You can also order through the Philip Allan Updates website: www.philipallan.co.uk

First printed 2009
Impression number   7
Year   2016

Illustrations: Jim Watson
Printed in India

Hachette UK's policy is to use papers that are natural, renewable and recyclable products and made from wood grown in sustainable forests. The logging and manufacturing processes are expected to conform to the environmental regulations of the country of origin.

P01974

Contents

Topic 6
Religion and young people

About this book

Revision is vital for success in your GCSE examination. No one can remember what they learned up to 2 years ago without a reminder. To be effective, revision must be planned. This book provides a carefully planned course of revision — here is how to use it.

The book	*The route to success*
Contents list	**Step 1** Check which topics you need to revise for your examination. Mark them clearly on the contents list and make sure you revise them.
Revision notes	**Step 2** Each section of the book gives you the facts you need to know for a topic. Read the notes carefully, and list the main points.
Key words	**Step 3** Key words are highlighted in the text and displayed in key word boxes. Learn them and their meanings. They must be used correctly in the examination.
Test yourself	**Step 4** A set of brief questions is given at the end of each section. Answer these to test how much you know. If you get one wrong, revise it again. You can try the questions before you start the topic to check what you know.
Examination questions	**Step 5** Examples of questions are given for you to practise. The more questions you practise, the better you will become at answering them.
Exam tips	**Step 6** The exam tips offer advice for achieving success. Read them and act on the advice when you answer the question.
Key word index	**Step 7** On page 63 there is a list of all the key words and the pages on which they appear. Use this index to check whether you know all the key words. This will help you to decide what you need to look at again.

Command words

All examination questions include **command** or **action** words. These tell you what the examiner wants you to do. Here are two of the most common ones:

- **Describe** — requires detail. For example, you may be asked to describe a birth ceremony in one religion that you have studied.
- **Explain** — here the examiner is expecting you to show understanding by giving reasons. For example, you may be asked to explain the importance of the birth ceremony you have described.

Revision rules

- Start early.

- Plan your time by making a timetable.

- Be realistic — don't try to do too much each night.

- Find somewhere quiet to work.

- Revise thoroughly — reading on its own is not enough.

- Summarise your notes, make headings for each topic.

- Ask someone to test you.

- Try to answer some questions from old papers. Your teacher will help you.

If there is anything you don't understand — ask your teacher.

Do you know?

- The exam board setting your paper?

- What level or tier you will be sitting?

- How many papers you will be taking?

- The date, time and place of each paper?

- How long each paper will be?

- What the subject of each paper will be?

- What the paper will look like? Do you write your answer on the paper or in a separate booklet?

- How many questions you should answer?

- Whether there is a choice of questions?

- Whether any part of the paper is compulsory?

If you don't know the answer to any of these questions as the exam approaches — ask your teacher.

Be prepared

The night before the exam

- Complete your final revision.

- Check the time and place of your examination.

- Get your pens ready.

- Go to bed early and set the alarm clock.

On the examination day

- Don't rush.

- Double check the time and place of your exam and your equipment.

- Arrive early.

- Keep calm — breathe deeply.

- Be positive.

Examination tips

- Keep calm and concentrate.

- Read the paper through before you start to write.

- Decide which questions you are going to answer.

- Make sure you can do all parts of the questions you choose.

- Complete all the questions that you have chosen.

- Don't spend too long on one question at the expense of the others.

- Read all questions carefully, then stick to the point and answer them fully.

- Use all your time.

- Check your answers.

- Do your best.

Topic 1
Religion and animal rights

Science shows that, genetically, there is little difference between a fruit fly and a human. The old idea that humans are far superior to all other creatures has been dealt a severe blow. Some would argue that humans are different from animals only in degree and not in kind. Many, however, would say that humans and apes have 99% of **DNA** in common, but that the 1% difference is crucial and that we are more than our DNA. They would argue that humans are able to make free (as opposed to learned) responses and are capable of abstract thinking. Nevertheless, many who believe that humans are different from animals in kind would still say that the rest of the created world should not be exploited or abused but be treated with respect.

The use and abuse of animals

In prehistoric times, animals were domesticated and used in several ways, notably for food. Over the centuries, the uses to which humans have put animals have increased enormously. In modern times, many people have become concerned that animals are being abused, and some would claim that at least the higher species have rights that humans should not infringe.

Factory farming of egg-laying hens

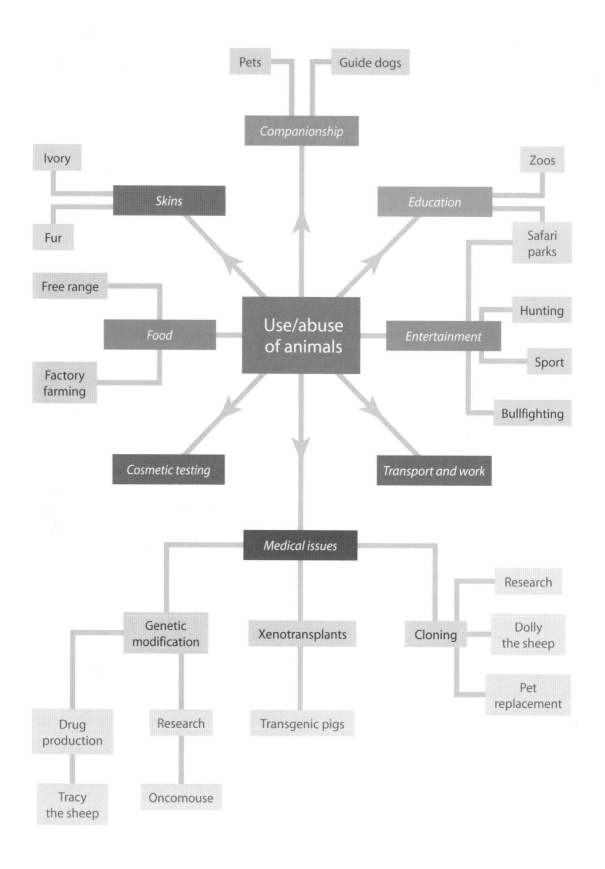

Pets

Guide dogs

Companionship

Ivory

Skins

Fur

Zoos

Education

Safari parks

Free range

Food

Factory farming

Use/abuse of animals

Entertainment

Hunting

Sport

Bullfighting

Cosmetic testing

Transport and work

Medical issues

Genetic modification

Xenotransplants

Cloning

Research

Dolly the sheep

Pet replacement

Drug production

Research

Transgenic pigs

Tracy the sheep

Oncomouse

Use of animals for food

There is much debate about this. UK law relating to farming practice, transporting animals for slaughter and the management of abattoirs is quite strict.

Vegetarians and **vegans** do not eat meat because:

- Rearing animals for food exploits them.
- Farming methods are often cruel.
- Humans do not need to eat meat: vegetarianism is a more healthy option.
- Less farmland is needed for feeding vegetarians; this would provide a solution to the global food shortage.
- Vegetarian food is safer: CJD is caused by eating animals infected with BSE.

Preservation of species from extinction

Throughout the world many species are endangered. It may be that many animals never discovered by humans are already extinct. There are many causes, including hunting for ivory and deforestation. Governments and animal charities are trying to halt **extinction** through a number of projects.

Wildlife parks

Zoos

Preservation of species

Education

Environmental improvements

Key words

Assisi Declarations

DNA

extinction

vegans

vegetarians

Elephants have to be protected against ivory traders and poachers

Fotolia

Religious attitudes to animals

In 1986, representatives from all religions met and came up with the **Assisi Declarations**: statements from each religion that the natural world, including animals, should be respected and conserved.

 ## Buddhism

- **First Precept** not to harm living things applies to animals
- Principles of **metta** (loving kindness) and **karuna** (compassion) affect treatment of animals
- Important to protect and live in harmony with the natural world
- To emulate the bee, which takes nectar without harming the flower (**Dhammapada** — sacred text — 49)
- Living sentient creatures should not be killed or harmed in any way (**Anchoranga Sutra** — sacred text)
- Interdependence of everything in natural world, so important to care for animals
- **Dalai Lama** opposed to animal experimentation
- Many believe that meat eating breaks the First Precept
- Others eat meat if offered, so as not to refuse what is a gift

 ## Case study

The Dalai Lama

- The religious and political leader of Tibetan Buddhists
- Since 1959 he has been leader of the Government of Tibet in Exile in India
- His views are respected by international politicians and religious leaders
- He has always promoted peaceful solutions to political and other problems and in 1989 was awarded the Nobel Peace Prize
- He has expressed his concerns about the threat to the environment and has campaigned for wildlife conservation

 ## Christianity

- God created animals and was pleased with his creation (Genesis 1) so humans should respect them
- Humans are **stewards** (guardians on behalf of God) not owners of creation, so should act responsibly

- Animals to be respected, but people should not treat them as equal to humans (Catechism of Catholic Church)
- A good person looks after his/her animals (Proverbs)
- Jesus' reference to God's care for sparrows extends to the rest of the created world
- God provides for the needs of animals as well as of humans (Psalm 104)
- **Francis of Assisi** patron saint of animals — Christians should follow his example
- RSPCA founded by Christians
- Many accept animal experimentation in medical research if no other alternative, but suffering to be kept to a minimum — encourage the three Rs (reduction, refinement, replacement)
- Most Christians prepared to eat meat as long as the animals have been treated kindly with good conditions and are killed humanely

 **Case study**

Francis of Assisi (1182–1226)

- Brought up in a wealthy family and led a life of luxury until a serious illness changed his perspective
- He became a wandering preacher and teacher, and he is seen as the founder of all the Franciscan orders of monks and nuns
- His love of nature and of animals led him to write the 'Canticle of the Sun', calling on the whole created world to join him in praising God
- He is said to have preached to hundreds of birds and befriended a wolf, and he created the first Christmas crib, using live animals
- He is the patron saint of ecology as well as of animals

 Hinduism

- Part of **dharma** (righteous living) to protect animals and uphold principle of **ahimsa** (no harm to any living thing)
- All creatures part of **Brahman** (ultimate reality) and of **samsara** (reincarnation) cycle, so should be respected
- Cows treated with special respect, as symbol of kindly quality of life
- Some animals associated with gods and **Ganesha** (god whose elephant head is a symbol of intelligence)
- **Vishnu** (god in form of preserver) took on form of animals to save world from danger
- Last of householder's five daily duties is to make offerings to all creatures
- Many are vegetarian because of ahimsa principle

Islam

- Animals part of **Allah**'s creation, so to be cared for
- Principle of **tawhid** (oneness of Allah) links all living things together
- Animals have feelings; their lives have a purpose in Allah's plan for his world (**Qur'an**)
- Animals to be killed humanely so no animal experimentation
- Animals have rights, so not to be used for human entertainment (though zoos allowed if purely for conservation of endangered species, as in the Arabian Oryx Project in Oman)
- Humans are **khalifahs** (stewards) not owners of creation and will be held to account (**akra** = accountability) for this on Judgement day
- Only **halal** meat to be eaten
- Carrion and pork are **haram** (not permitted)

Judaism

- God created animals and was pleased with his creation (Genesis 1) so humans should respect them
- Humans are stewards not owners of creation, so should act responsibly
- A good person looks after his/her animals (Proverbs)
- God provides for the needs of animals as well as of humans (Psalm 104)
- **Noachide commandments** (rules said to have been given to Noah) forbid cruelty to animals — these laws are binding on all humanity, not just Jews

The Arabian Oryx Project has re-established an oryx population in the wild

Fotolia

- **Fourth Commandment (Shabbat)** applies to animals as well as humans
- Killing to be humane, according to **shechitah** rituals (method of slaughter laid down in Jewish law)
- **Kosher** (Jewish rules stating what is permissible) rules to be obeyed — some animal meat (e.g. pork) **treifa**, i.e. forbidden, and meat not to be mixed with dairy

Sikhism

- God created and provides for animals, so we should be kind to them
- Humans are custodians of the earth; should treat animals with respect
- Accountable to God for treatment of created world — care of animals part of dharma
- Some **Gurus** (spiritual teachers) famous for hunting
- **Guru Nanak** (founder of Sikhism) taught that all foods are pure, so those who eat meat can eat all types
- Some Sikhs are vegetarian
- **Langar** food (food provided in gurdwaras — Sikh places of worship) always vegetarian

Key words	
Buddhism	haram
Anchoranga Sutra	khalifah
Dalai Lama	Qur'an
Dhammapada	tawhid
First Precept	**Judaism**
metta	Fourth Commandment (Shabbat)
karuna	
Christianity	kosher
Francis of Assisi	Noachide commandments
stewards	
Hinduism	shechitah
ahimsa	treifa
Brahman	**Sikhism**
dharma	Gurus
Ganesha	Guru Nanak
samsara	langar
Vishnu	
Islam	
akra	
Allah	
halal	

Test yourself

1 Indicate whether each of the following statements is true or false:

	TRUE	FALSE
There is a big genetic difference between apes and humans.	☐	☐
Vegans eat meat.	☐	☐
There are strict rules in the UK governing the slaughter of animals.	☐	☐
Religious leaders produced environmental statements known as the Assisi Declarations.	☐	☐
One charity that cares for animals is the NSPCC.	☐	☐
Deforestation is a major cause of the extinction of animal species.	☐	☐

2 Explain the attitudes of religious believers towards animals. Refer to one or more religions in your answer.

Examination question

'Everyone should be vegetarian.'

Do you agree? Give reasons for your answer, showing that you have thought about more than one point of view. Refer to religious arguments in your answer.

(6 marks)

Exam tip

Ensure that you understand beliefs and teachings from the religion(s) you have studied on every topic set for study. It may help you when you are revising to have a postcard for each topic. Note down four religious beliefs or teachings relating to each of the topics.

Topic 2
Religion and planet earth

The environment

In recent decades most people have become increasingly aware of the wonders of the universe and in particular of the fragility and beauty of planet earth. Religious believers in particular view planet earth with a mixture of awe and wonder.

Fotolia

Religious views about the origins of life

 Buddhism

- No creation stories as Buddha felt only intellectually limited people asked such questions
- No simple answer that is right for everyone
- The world follows a cycle marked by decay, dissolution and rebirth

Christianity

- According to Genesis 1, the world was created in 6 days in an orderly fashion, beginning with light and then everything that was needed to sustain life, and climaxing with the creation of humanity
- Genesis 2 describes the creation of man from the earth, the Garden of Eden, the animals and birds, and finally Eve from the man's rib
- Most Christians view these stories as myths, i.e. stories containing deep truths about the purpose and meaning of life
- Some Christians believe that Genesis 1 gives a true account of what happened, but that it was in six stages rather than six 24-hour periods, and that the verse about God saying 'Let there be light' refers in fact to the Big Bang

 # Hinduism

- There are various creation stories depicting a cycle of development, dissolution and recreation
- According to one story, Vishnu, asleep on a cobra floating on an ocean, was awakened by the **Aum** (sacred symbol and sound representing God) sound; a lotus flower grew out of his navel and out of it came **Brahma** (God as creator), who then split the flower to form the heavens, the earth and the skies. He then created everything on the earth

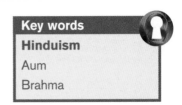

Key words
Hinduism
Aum
Brahma

 # Islam

- There is no specific creation story but there are some similarities to the Genesis stories of Judaism/Christianity: the world created in 6 days (Surah 11:7) and the story of Adam and Hawa as the ancestors of all humanity (Surah 2:30–39)
- Allah the sole creator of everything

 # Judaism

- According to Genesis 1, the world was created in 6 days in an orderly fashion, beginning with light and then everything needed to sustain life, and climaxing with the creation of humanity
- Genesis 2 describes the creation of man from the earth, the Garden of Eden, the animals and birds, and finally Eve from the man's rib
- Many Jews view these stories as myth, i.e. they are stories that contain deep truths about the meaning and purpose of life

Sikhism

- No specific creation story but beliefs contained in hymns of praise
- For billions of years, only God existed; then from nothing he made everything in the universe
- Only God knows everything

Environmental problems

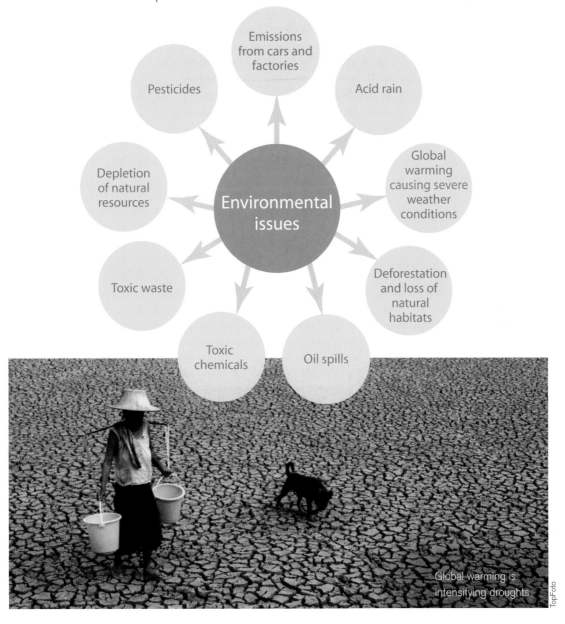

- Emissions from cars and factories
- Pesticides
- Acid rain
- Depletion of natural resources
- Environmental issues
- Global warming causing severe weather conditions
- Toxic waste
- Deforestation and loss of natural habitats
- Toxic chemicals
- Oil spills

Global warming is intensifying droughts

TopFoto

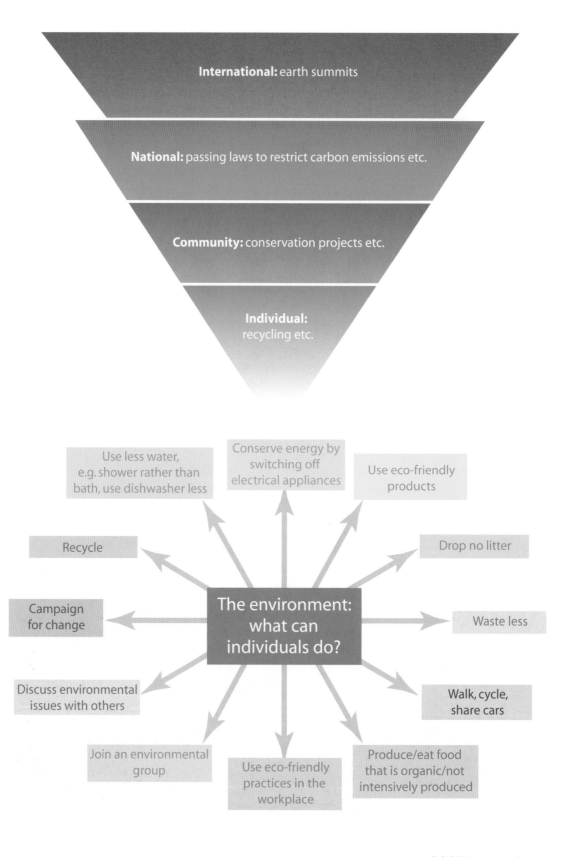

International: earth summits

National: passing laws to restrict carbon emissions etc.

Community: conservation projects etc.

Individual: recycling etc.

Use less water, e.g. shower rather than bath, use dishwasher less

Conserve energy by switching off electrical appliances

Use eco-friendly products

Recycle

Drop no litter

Campaign for change

The environment: what can individuals do?

Waste less

Discuss environmental issues with others

Walk, cycle, share cars

Join an environmental group

Use eco-friendly practices in the workplace

Produce/eat food that is organic/not intensively produced

Religious attitudes to the environment

All religions emphasise the following principles:

- Responsibility: humans are accountable for how they treat the world.
- **Stewardship**: humans are not owners of planet earth, but have the sacred duty of caring for it.
- **Justice** entails fair treatment, i.e. humans have to practise conservation and those living in the developed world have a duty to use the earth's resources wisely, with the interests and rights of both those in LEDCs (less economically developed countries) and future generations in mind

In 1986 representatives from all religions met and came up with the Assisi Declarations — statements from each religion that the natural world should be respected and conserved.

 ## Buddhism

- Important to protect and live in harmony with the natural world
- Humans to emulate the bee, which takes nectar without harming the flower (Dhammapada 49), by taking what they need without damaging the universe
- Interdependence of everything in the natural world, and human actions make it what it is
- Monks and nuns taught not to destroy plants or trees

Gandan monastery, Mongolia

- Involved in projects organised by ARC (Alliance of Religions and Conservation, founded as a result of Assisi Declarations) and the WWF (World Wildlife Fund)
- Reintroduced former ban on hunting the snow leopard and saiga antelope (both endangered species)
- Seen as expression of karuna
- Encourages Buddhists to be involved in sustainable natural resource management
- Seven traditional Buddhist sacred reserves recreated

✝ Christianity

- In **harvest festival** services Christians acknowledge God as the Creator
- Humans have great power, which must be used responsibly
- The concept of sanctity of life extends beyond humans
- Many churches are becoming eco-friendly, i.e. supporting the environment, with strict policies on use of energy etc.
- Major aid agencies are involved with environmental issues because of the link with global poverty, and there are many Christian environmental agencies

Christians attend services to thank God for the harvest

A ROCHA
Caring for God's world together

- Christian environmental organisation
- Started in Portugal (where A Rocha means 'the rock') in 1983
- Now spread to five continents
- Has projects in 18 countries and takes on volunteer workers
- Concerned with conservation and saving species from extinction
- Building up of eco-tourist industry in Kenya has led to better provision of secondary education in its coastal region
- A 260-metre suspended walkway, which goes through a mangrove forest to a bird-hide, was opened in 2003 and over 1,000 tourists have used it
- The proceeds from this have been used for bursaries to enable over 90 children to attend 30 different secondary schools around the country

 Hinduism

- Brahman in everything, so planet earth to be treated with utmost respect
- Protection of environment part of dharma
- All living things bound together because of samsara
- Well-being of human race dependent on right attitudes to planet earth and its resources
- There is a saying that the earth is our mother and that we are her children

Chipko Movement

- Known as 'tree hugging' movement
- Started with women surrounding trees to stop them being felled in the Himalayan region, because of concerns about erosion
- Extended to many other provinces
- Led to many bans on deforestation
- Inspired programmes concerned with water management, energy conservation and recycling and led to detailed environmental studies

Islam

- Allah's creation, so should be respected and conserved
- Created with a natural balance (**fitrah**) but human greed has upset balance and increased scale of natural disasters (which occurred before as beneficial to the earth's well-being)
- As khalifahs, humans should use resources responsibly, remembering that they will be accountable (akra)
- Concept of **hima** (undeveloped land left for pasture) extended to conservation of forests and other resources

Misali fishing communities

- Dynamite fishing was destroying the turtle population and the coral reef
- Islanders ignored information leaflets, threats from government and ban on dynamite fishing
- Muslim leaders of the communities on Misali Island came together with ARC, the Islamic Foundation for Ecology and Environmental Science and other groups to study Islamic environmental teachings
- Concluded that dynamite fishing was contrary to Islamic law

Judaism

- Genesis stories emphasise the goodness of the universe, i.e. its fitness for God's purposes
- Genesis 2 states that humans are meant to work the earth and care for it
- Old Testament rule was to let land lie fallow every 7 years
- Responsible stewardship means enjoying but not exploiting resources
- Reference in **Talmud** (commentary by rabbis on the Torah) to surrounding cities with a ring of trees; trees being planted again in modern Israel
- Jewish businesses to deal with waste efficiently, according to Talmud's rules

Hava and Adam ecological farm in Modi'in, Israel

- 5-month Eco-Israel project for English-speaking young Jewish adults
- Developing self-reliant community with Israeli volunteers, based on ecological principles
- Farming according to Jewish cycles, seasons and the Hebrew calendar
- Developing new land ethic

Sikhism

- Universe created by God and God is in all things, so planet earth to be respected
- Humans to act as its custodians, using their greater power responsibly
- God-given duty to protect planet earth

Sikh Gurdwara Project

- 28,000 gurdwaras in India
- Heavy use of fossil fuels to provide daily food for poor in langars
- Gurdwaras have committed themselves to being more eco-conscious
- Intending to use solar power in Delhi's eight largest gurdwaras and to fit fuel-efficient cooking equipment in rural gurdwaras
- Would reduce energy consumption by up to 15%

Test yourself

1 Fill in the gaps in the chart below

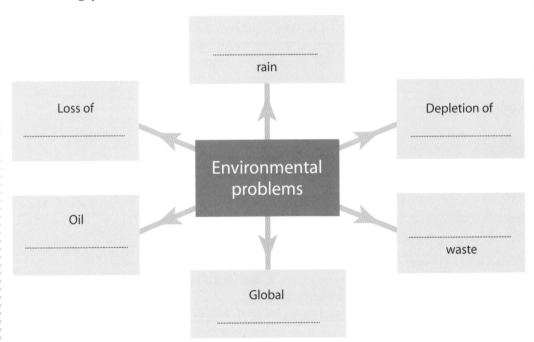

2 What forms of international action are being taken to conserve the world?
3 What can the UK government do to conserve resources?
4 How can local communities be involved in conservation?

Examination question

a Explain how individual religious believers might be involved in conserving the environment. *(6 marks)*

b Explain why religious believers think that it is important to conserve the environment. *(6 marks)*

Exam tip

Read the question very carefully. If the trigger word is 'explain', note whether it is a 'how' or 'why' question. Many marks are lost in exams through candidates explaining how, when they are required to explain why, and vice versa.

Religion and prejudice

Prejudice and discrimination

Prejudice seems to go back to the beginning of history and continues to be a major problem. Even though many might deny it, most if not all people have some prejudices. Some prejudices may be trivial, e.g. feeling dislike for a food without knowing anything about it, but others are more serious, particularly when they lead to **discrimination**. They cause untold misery for the victims.

Prejudice refers to what goes on in the mind. It consists of pre-judging, i.e. holding fixed views on someone or something without good reason. Prejudiced views are irrational, e.g. thinking that all women are bad drivers.

Discrimination is putting prejudice into action. It is treating someone in a particular way (usually negatively) without good reason, e.g. refusing to employ someone as a taxi driver because she is a woman.

Causes of prejudice and discrimination

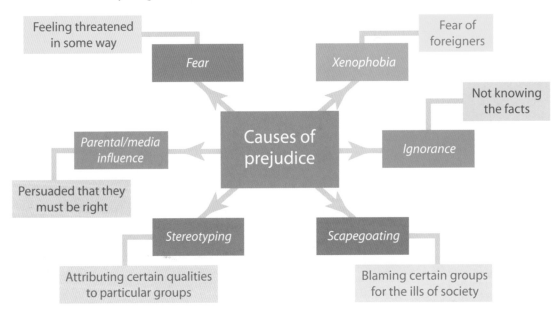

Types of prejudice and discrimination

- colour and race — particularly towards black people
- religion — often towards Muslims
- gender — usually towards women
- disability — towards people with mental or physical disability
- class — e.g. upper classes vs working classes
- lifestyle — e.g. towards travellers
- looks — e.g. towards those with birthmarks

Key words

discrimination
institutional racism
prejudice
scapegoating
stereotyping
xenophobia

The success of Dame Tanni Grey-Thompson has helped raise the profile of athletes with disabilities

Many forms of discrimination are illegal. The law covers many areas, including employment, education, benefits, housing. It also deals with verbal discrimination, e.g. the kind of speech that might encourage racial hatred, verbal harassment of female employees by employers. Victims of discrimination can take their case to tribunal. But discrimination continues to be a major problem in the UK because the law cannot dictate how people think. It cannot prosecute prejudice, and prejudice quickly spills over into action. The law may also not be able to give protection if:

- the discrimination is very subtle
- there are no witnesses
- witnesses are afraid to give evidence
- the victim does not report anything for fear of what will follow
- the victim is not as articulate or well represented legally as the discriminator
- there is **institutional racism** as, for example, was seen to be the case in the Stephen Lawrence murder investigation

Stephen Lawrence

Religious attitudes to prejudice and discrimination

 **Buddhism**

- Buddha rejected caste system of Hinduism
- Of six mental delusions, ignorance is the major cause of prejudice and greed, anger and pride contribute
- The Buddha taught that love conquers hate
- Recognising equal status of all increases good kamma
- Right speech and right action rule out prejudice and discrimination
- The Buddha taught equality of all in the **Sangha** (Buddhist community) and ordained women, despite social conditions in India
- Buddhist nuns in many countries

 **Christianity**

- Prejudice and discrimination are sinful
- According to the Bible all people are children of God and should be given the respect and dignity their status as human beings deserves
- Jesus healed Jews and non-Jews, men and women and people with disabilities; he made friends with those who were despised
- In his parable of the Good Samaritan, the despised Samaritan, and not the Jewish religious leaders, was the one to help the injured Jew
- All human beings have the same right to fair and equal treatment
- **Ordination** (making someone a priest) of women in many Protestant churches; Roman Catholic Church and some Anglican churches do not accept women priests, claiming it is not discrimination but difference of role
- Women may become nuns in Roman Catholic and Anglican denominations

 **Hinduism**

- All living things contain **atman** (ultimate reality as individual self), so all equal
- **Caste** system (division into social groups) made illegal in India in 1948; **Dalits** (traditionally beneath the lowest caste) have right to education and to vote
- Caste system still strong in traditional Hindu families and in some remote rural areas, especially in relation to marriage; low caste seen as due to sins of past life
- Men and women equal, but have different roles: women traditionally the homemakers and performers of **puja** (worship in the home)

- Boys tend to take priority in education in India but that is slowly changing and, in the UK, good education is a priority for all

Islam

- Allah sole creator of all, so all humans equal, regardless of status
- Equality on **hajj** (pilgrimage to Makkah) — all male pilgrims wear **ihram** (simple white garment) and women dress in plain clothing
- The concept of **ummah** (brotherhood of all Muslims) stresses racial equality of all
- Equality of men and women although roles different; women have many rights, e.g. to study, own property, inherit
- Modest clothing (**hijab**) intended to liberate women, not constrain them

Judaism

- All humanity created in image of God
- Torah commands that all foreigners be treated with respect and compassion, e.g. corn/fruit dropped during harvesting to be left for poor and foreigners to pick up
- Election of Jews not privilege but responsibility — to bring humanity to God
- J-CORE brings black, Asian and Jewish communities together in joint projects to create harmony and promote equality of opportunity
- Orthodox Jews see women as equal but with different roles: **Bat Chayil** rather than **Bat Mitzvah** (see Topic 6); the woman the homemaker and responsible for religious education of young children
- Reform Judaism allows for equality of roles, e.g. women **rabbis** (Jewish religious leaders)

Sikhism

- All humans are children of God: differences in colour, race, gender etc. are meaningless
- Gurus condemned caste system in India
- Equality of all in langar (dining hall found in every gurdwara); serving of vegetarian food means no one feels excluded
- Women may become **Khalsa Sikhs** (fully initiated Sikhs) and **granthis** (officials at gurdwara)
- In gurdwara, everyone sitting on floor as sign of equal status; separation of men from women simply to prevent distraction or accidental contact with someone else's spouse

Key words	
Buddhism	**Judaism**
Sangha	Bat Chayil
Christianity	Bat Mitzvah
Ordination	rabbi
Hinduism	**Sikhism**
atman	granthi
caste	Khalsa Sikh
Dalits	
puja	
Islam	
hajj	
hijab	
ihram	
ummah	

By word: in sermons and speeches, by refusing to join in racist conversation	By example: parents and other adults setting a good example

How can religious believers counter prejudice and discrimination?

By action: protest marches, writing to MPs, befriending vulnerable groups	By showing tolerance, justice and encouraging harmony

Test yourself

Case study

Martin Luther King

- Born in the USA in 1929 — a black American
- Became a Baptist minister and the leader of the black community in his town
- Led the bus boycott in 1955 after Rosa Parkes was arrested for refusing to give up her seat on the bus to a white man, and this resulted in desegregation of buses
- Became leader of the civil rights movement — involved in a wide variety of non-violent protests that led gradually to desegregation of schools, restaurants etc.
- Despite threats to his life and a bomb left outside his house, he constantly advocated non-violence — the only way to neutralise evil was by responding to it with love
- He stressed Jesus' teaching: 'Love your enemies and pray for those who persecute you'

Martin Luther King

- He claimed that violence does not express the love of God; it only expresses hatred
- The Ku Klux Klan created widespread terror with their attacks on black communities, which led to some black people rejecting Martin Luther King's non-violent stance
- Gave the 'I have a dream speech' at a huge rally in Washington, speaking of his dream that one day all races, religions etc. would live together in harmony
- Awarded the Nobel Peace Prize in 1964
- Black people given the vote in 1965
- Assassinated in 1968

1 Name ways in which black people suffered discrimination in the USA in the twentieth century.

2 Explain why many people still admire Martin Luther King

3 'Christians should never use violence to stop discrimination.' What do you think? Explain your opinion.

Examination question

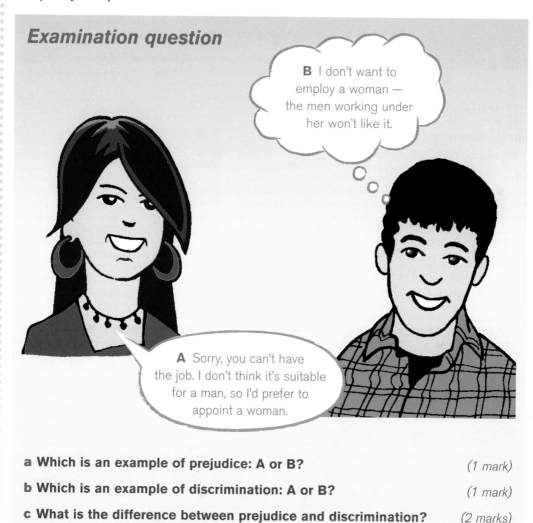

B I don't want to employ a woman — the men working under her won't like it.

A Sorry, you can't have the job. I don't think it's suitable for a man, so I'd prefer to appoint a woman.

a Which is an example of prejudice: A or B? *(1 mark)*

b Which is an example of discrimination: A or B? *(1 mark)*

c What is the difference between prejudice and discrimination? *(2 marks)*

d Explain religious attitudes to prejudice and discrimination. Refer to one religion in your answer. *(6 marks)*

Exam tip

If stimulus material is given at the start of a question, do look at it carefully and make good use of it in the exam question. It is not just decoration or included to fill in a space.

Religion and early life

The miracle of life

Whatever their religious beliefs and regardless of whether they want to have children themselves, many people feel awe and wonder at the mystery of life. They refer to it as a miracle. Many would also say that children are a blessing and couples suffer terribly if they find they are infertile. **Abortion** is not a trivial matter.

'Your body is a temple of the Holy Spirit'

Sanctity of life

Life is a gift from God — to be treasured

Life is infinitely precious

Many people see children as a blessing

When does life begin?

Biological life begins with the fertilisation of the egg by the sperm, but what is meant here is at what stage is it meaningful life, i.e. life with rights? There are different views on this:

- At conception
  - the **pro-life** view
  - from the moment of fertilisation, a new person with potential, a human being complete with a soul, has come into existence
- At birth
  - the **pro-choice** view
  - independent life only starts at birth; until that point the foetus is totally dependent on the mother
- **Viability**
  - the view taken by the law
  - the foetus has rights from the point at which, if born, it could have a reasonable chance of survival (currently taken to be 24 weeks)
- A gradual process
  - the view of many religious believers
  - the embryo has the right to respect from conception, but full rights are acquired as the foetus develops (e.g. development of the nervous system, brain activity)

Abortion

Abortion is the deliberate termination of pregnancy. It is permitted under UK law, provided certain conditions are met. The cut-off point for most abortions is 24 weeks.

UK law

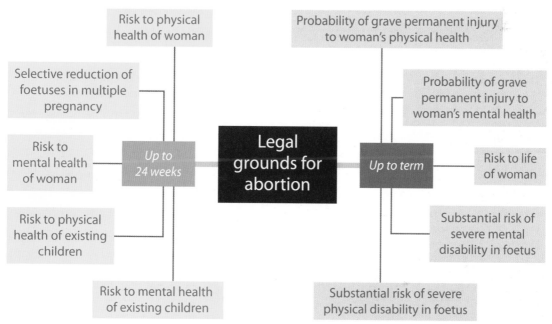

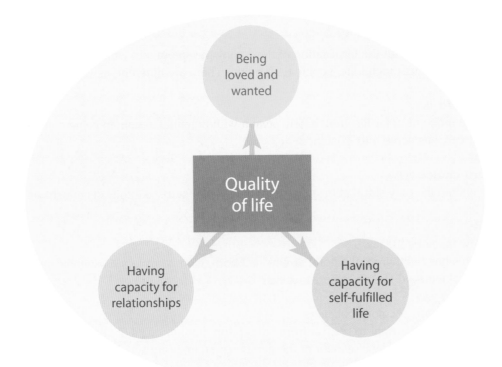

Secular arguments for and against abortion

For	Against
No child should be unwanted	No child need be unwanted — there are alternatives to abortion
The **embryo/foetus** is just a clump of cells — it is at best a potential life	Life begins at **conception**, when something totally and uniquely new comes into being
A young girl is not ready for the responsibilities of motherhood	A young girl is not mature enough to deal with any long-lasting guilt feelings after abortion
It is cruel to make a raped woman go through with pregnancy	It is wrong to punish a child for the father's action
Aborting a disabled foetus is in the best interests of everyone	It is wrong for those without disability to make quality of life judgements about people with disability
The right to **autonomy** — the mother has the right to choose for herself	The right to autonomy should be limited as in this case the mother is making choices for someone else (i.e. the foetus)
The woman knows what is best for herself and the foetus	The woman's emotional state may cloud her judgement

Pro-choice

Maternal rights come first

She is more fully alive than a foetus

She should decide what happens in and to her body

Neil Bromhall/SPL

Pro-life

Foetal rights come first

The foetus is fully alive as a human being with potential

The foetus is vulnerable and needs protection

A 5-month old foetus in the womb

Alternatives to abortion

- the mother keeping the baby
- **fostering** until the mother can care for the baby herself
- **adoption**

Pro-life

- (+) The baby's right to life is respected
- (+) The mother will not suffer the guilt feelings that are common after abortion
- (+) As well as support from the state, many church organisations will give her all the financial and emotional support she and her baby need
- (+) Infertile couples are given great joy and the child has a loving home

Pro-life

- (−) The mother and baby might struggle throughout life without access to support
- (−) The child might spend his/her whole childhood in foster care because the mother is not ready for the responsibility but does not want the child to be adopted and he/she may feel unwanted by the mother
- (−) There may be emotional problems later for all concerned when an adopted child wants to find his/her mother

Religious beliefs for and against abortion

Buddhism

- Traditionalists think abortion is wrong as life begins at conception, so it breaks First Precept
- Mother and abortionist acquire bad kamma
- But in some situations, in best interests of foetus (e.g. severe disability)
- Dalai Lama stated that situations should be taken into account
- Metta, karuna and right intention should underlie decisions
- Above all, a personal decision

Christianity

Roman Catholic Church

- Abortion is a grave sin tantamount to murder, incurring **excommunication** (not allowed to receive Holy Communion)
- Human being with potential — the embryo has full rights from the start
- Embryo absolutely defenceless — merits special protection
- Infinitely precious to God; sanctity of life
- All life has potential and is of equal value — not for humans to pass judgement on quality of life for foetus with disability
- Wrong to punish child for father's sin in case of rape — birth of child is good coming out of evil
- Unwanted child can be adopted — brings joy to infertile couples and chance of life and love for child
- Practical and emotional support given by Roman Catholic community and charities can enable young mothers to cope

NB Some Protestants hold these views

Anglican Church

- Abortion is a great moral evil — concern about number of abortions taking place
- Life is sacred and the foetus deserves respect and protection
- But in certain circumstances, abortion may be lesser of two evils, e.g. to save mother's life; in cases of extreme distress such as rape
- Late abortions (i.e. after 24 weeks) for disability — only where child would die soon after birth
- Abortions up to 24 weeks for disability if in child's best interests
- Importance of compassion and love for all concerned
- A matter for personal decision, in accordance with conscience
- Tries to balance sanctity of life with quality of life

Methodist Church

- Similar to Anglican view — undesirable, but sometimes lesser of two evils
- Justified in some cases — risk to life/health of mother and existing family, extreme poverty, rape, severe disability

Hinduism

- Permissible only where mother's life at risk
- Dharma at householder stage to rear children
- Goes against principle of ahimsa (doing no harm); atman present from conception
- Stops foetus moving closer to **moksha** (release from samsara)
- But female foeticide (killing of foetus) is an issue in India because of dowries
- Some accept abortion in cases of rape, disability, other risks to maternal health

Islam

- Permissible at any stage if risk to mother's life; loss of mother affects society more than loss of foetus
- Otherwise haram (forbidden) for most Muslims
- Strong opposition to excuse of poverty; Qur'an teaches that Allah will provide for the poor, so abortion shows lack of trust
- Dispute over time of ensoulment: official view places it at 120 days and until then mother's rights take priority
- Some place it at 40 days or at conception
- 1990 meeting of World Islamic League: permissible before 120 days for severe disability
- Minority accept it in cases of rape or incest
- Stress on sanctity of life and compassion

Judaism

- Importance of sanctity of life
- Foetus not a person until born; no human rights until head born — up to that moment, abortion permissible to save woman's life, but from then on foetus has equal rights with mother
- Exodus 21:22 often seen as showing difference in moral status between mother and foetus
- Abortion to save maternal life a duty, though rabbi should be consulted; often extended to include suicidal mother
- Tiny minority accept it for disability out of concern for maternal mental health

Sikhism

- Human life begins at conception, so abortion an insult to the Creator
- Stress on sanctity of life
- Infanticide banned for Khalsa Sikhs in the **Reht Maryada** (Sikh code of conduct) and most extend this to include abortion
- Most accept it if a risk to mother's life
- A minority accept it in cases of rape
- Grounds of disability not accepted
- Female foeticide strongly condemned

Test yourself

Case study

Joanna Jepson

- Born in 1976
- An Anglican priest
- Had many years of operations to correct a jaw defect, for which she had suffered bullying at school
- Has a brother who has Down's Syndrome
- In 2001 she took the West Mercia police to court for not investigating the late abortion of a foetus with a cleft palate — she regarded this as unlawful killing
- Her complaint was dismissed
- Sometimes a cleft palate can be an indication of far more serious problems with the foetus, but in this case, Joanna Jepson claimed that this was not so

Joanna Jepson

1 What is meant by the term abortion?

2 Which particular part of the abortion law did the case brought by Joanna Jepson relate to?

3 Give two reasons why her views on abortion might be affected by her personal experiences.

4 What is meant by pro-life and pro-choice?

5 Explain two answers that are given to the question of when meaningful life begins.

Examination question

Explain the difference between sanctity and quality of life. *(3 marks)*

Explain why some religious believers might support abortion in some cases. *(4 marks)*

'Any action to prevent the birth of an unwanted child is the most loving thing to do.'

Do you agree? Give reasons for your answer, showing that you have thought about more than one point of view. Refer to religious arguments in your answer. *(6 marks)*

Exam tip

In answering 6-mark evaluation questions, ensure that you include religious arguments in your answer. A purely secular (non-religious) answer will not receive more than 3 marks. To gain full marks, there needs to be clear reference to religious arguments.

Religion, war and peace

Causes and consequences of war

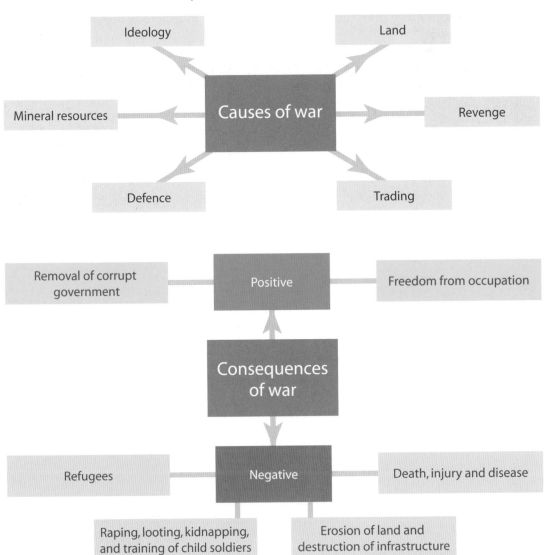

TopFoto

One result of war is that many people have to flee from their homes

Types of warfare

There are a number of different types of warfare that have been used in the twentieth and twenty-first centuries:

- Conventional. This covers a wide range of weaponry, including guns, laser guided missiles, cluster bombs and land mines. The UK army no longer uses land mines as they cause death and terrible injuries to innocent civilians.
- Chemical. This is banned by the Geneva Conventions (international rules intended to prevent inhumanity in war) but nevertheless chemical warfare has been used, e.g. by the USA in the Vietnam War. These weapons can cause choking, severe vomiting, paralysis, terrible burns and blindness.
- Biological. This type of warfare has also been banned by the Geneva Conventions, but is nevertheless being developed in a number of countries. One example would be releasing anthrax into the atmosphere.
- Nuclear. The first example of **nuclear warfare** was in August 1945 when the USA dropped atomic bombs on Hiroshima and Nagasaki in Japan. Thousands died immediately and many more thousands died slowly from the effects of radiation. Still today, people are dying of cancers related to the dropping of those bombs.

The atomic bomb on Hiroshima completely destroyed the city

Many nations, including the UK, have nuclear weapons. They see them as a deterrent: possession of them protects them from attack. Some other nations are in the process of developing nuclear technology, which is a cause of concern. **Nuclear proliferation** might lead to irresponsible leaders or terrorists obtaining such weapons and using them. Some Christians join CND, which is an organisation that campaigns to get rid of nuclear weapons in all countries, including the UK.

Terrorism

This is the often indiscriminate use of violence to achieve particular political or religious goals, to redress injustice or to overthrow a regime. Whatever the motive, **terrorism** is aimed at creating an atmosphere of fear and putting pressure on those in power.

A common form of terrorism is suicide bombing and those who die in this way are regarded as martyrs. Terrorists justify their actions as a last resort: they are seen as the only way of making people listen to their grievances. Most people, however, condemn all acts of terrorism, claiming that they show a total disregard for life and can never be justified.

A CND member campaigning on the 60th anniversary of the Hiroshima bomb

GCSE Revision Guide

The Just War theory

The **Just War theory** refers to the belief that war is never a good thing, but sometimes it may be justified as the lesser of two evils. It is a very ancient theory, but was developed over the centuries by great thinkers in the Roman Catholic Church. Some politicians and journalists use it when assessing whether or not conflict is justified. For a war to be declared just, eight criteria are taken into account. Hinduism, Islam, Judaism and Sikhism have their own versions.

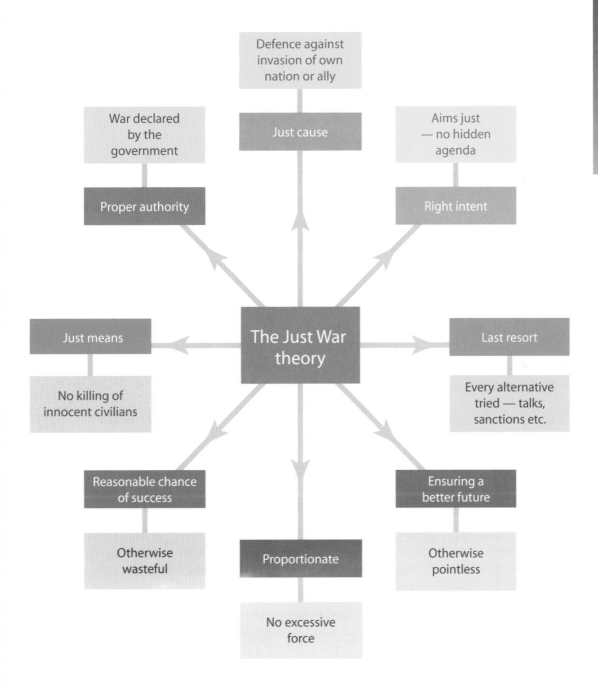

Pacifism

This is the belief that violence against other human beings can never be justified. War is always wrong and it can never be the lesser of two evils. There are strong arguments both for and against **pacifism**.

Arguments for pacifism	Arguments against pacifism
Beliefs about human life ■ everyone has the right to life ■ life is sacred ■ lives should be treated with respect ■ all are brothers and sisters	**The right to life is not absolute** ■ an aggressor has forfeited that right by the act of aggression ■ some lives may be sacrificed to protect others
War causes immense suffering ■ modern methods in particular harm the innocent ■ the suffering caused is out of all proportion to the evil being fought ■ the emotional suffering may affect future generations	**The Just War conditions** ■ seek to protect the innocent ■ ensure proportionality in violence ■ refusal to fight may make aggressors think they can do whatever they want, which may result in more suffering. It is important to defend and protect the innocent and sometimes this can be done only through war
War is a waste of resources ■ the money spent in the UK on weapons would solve social and global problems ■ money should be spent on saving lives, not destroying them ■ it causes irreparable damage to the environment ■ it uses up minerals and other resources	**War can be a wise use of resources** ■ wars that are fought to end injustice may save money and resources in the long run as greedy oppressors waste resources even more
War encourages undesirable attitudes ■ e.g. greed, hatred, prejudice, lust for power, arrogance	**War brings out the best in people** ■ e.g. courage, comradeship, compassion, humility, desire for justice

Peacekeepers

Sometimes, when a truce has been signed between two sides in a war, the **United Nations** or NATO will send in peacekeeping forces. These consist of soldiers from a wide range of nations, whose role it is to prevent conflict starting up again, revenge attacks etc. The soldiers are lightly armed for the purposes of self-defence.

A current example of peacekeeping forces can be seen in two African nations: Chad and the Central African Republic. Their main aim is to create a secure environment to which refugees can return and live safely.

Peacemakers

Christian Peacemaker Teams (CPT) was founded over 20 years ago to encourage a non-violent alternative to war. Norman Kember went with a CPT group to Iraq, to protest against the US led invasion of that country. He wished to show his support for the ordinary Iraqi people and to encourage peace. In the autumn of 2005 he was seized with others and kept as a hostage. One of his colleagues was killed by the kidnappers, but some months later Kember was located and freed by British armed forces.

Norman Kember

Case study

The International Federation of the Red Cross and the Red Crescent

- Started off as the Red Cross in 1863 by a Swiss businessman who was horrified by the thousands of men simply left to die after the Battle of Solferino
- Responsible for the first Geneva Convention
- Red Cross groups founded in many different countries, e.g. the British Red Cross founded in the late nineteenth century
- During the Second World War, the Red Cross sent parcels of food, clothes, letters from home etc. to those captured and held in camps as prisoners of war by the Germans
- Developed into an international organisation in the twentieth century, bringing together the Red Cross and the Red Crescent
- Many organisations form part of this International Federation, e.g. the British Red Cross, the Algerian Red Crescent
- Cares for the injured on the battlefield
- Provides for the needs of refugees

Key words

Just War theory

nuclear warfare

nuclear proliferation

pacifism

terrorism

United Nations

Religious views on war and pacifism

 ## Buddhism

- The Buddha taught that greatness consists in keeping the First Precept
- Harmonious living is purpose of life; conflict is result of ignorance

- Non-violence essential to building up good kamma
- Concept of collective kamma: national well-being dependent on government that promotes peace — this is achieved by using **skilful means**
- Right livelihood prohibits involvement in production/distribution of weapons
- Dalai Lama won Nobel Peace Prize for seeking peace; against use of violence; right weapons are truth, courage and determination
- Most Buddhists are pacifist, though some Buddhist countries have armies for self-defence

 Christianity

- All Christians stress the importance of **reconciliation**, **forgiveness**, justice and **peace**
- The different views of Christians do not coincide with differences in denominations, i.e. some Roman Catholics, Anglicans and Methodists are pacifist and some are not
- The Society of Friends (Quakers) is the only denomination that is officially pacifist
- There are many Christian pacifist groups, e.g. Pax Christi
- Christian pacifists refer to the teaching of Jesus
    - love your enemies and pray for your persecutors
    - those who live by the sword die by the sword
- Christians who are not pacifist tend to agree with the approach of the Just War theory
- They claim that the teaching and example of Jesus were unrelated to issues of war and peace and should not be taken literally or distorted
- St Paul told Christians to obey rulers because they were given their authority from God
- The Catechism of the Catholic Church supports the Just War theory, accepting that war may occasionally be a 'necessary evil'
- Pope John XXIII spoke out against nuclear weapons in 1963

 Hinduism

- Good karma is built up by ahimsa and **satyagraha** (Gandhi's non-violent policy of 'the force of truth')
- **Gandhi** (Indian religious and political leader) stated that an eye for an eye would make the whole world blind
- Accept **dharma yuddha** (form of Just War) if:
    - country is invaded
    - illegal coup has taken place
    - people are exploited or oppressed
- Restrictions on the kind of warfare/weapons, and civilians/those who have surrendered are not to be harmed

★ **Islam**

- Concept of peace central to Islam
- **Lesser jihad** (jihad means 'struggle') is military jihad and **harb al-muqadis** (holy war) is fought to enable Muslims to practise faith freely
- Rules of lesser jihad
  - to be declared and led by religious leader
  - just cause: in name of Allah and according to his will
  - in defence of tribe or country against oppression
  - aimed at achieving good, not evil
  - last resort
  - enemies to be treated humanely and no vengeance after end of conflict
  - no indiscriminate killing, and trees, crops and animals to be protected
- Martyrdom rewarded with paradise

✡ **Judaism**

- Concept of peace central: according to Talmud, world built on pillars of justice, truth and peace
- **Messianic era** (the age ruled by the Messiah, a religious figure awaited by many Jews) seen as time of peace and harmony
- Encouragement to move towards nuclear disarmament
- **Milchemet mitzvah** (obligatory war)
  - a holy war resulting from God's command
  - in defence of lives
  - to prevent imminent invasion
  - to help country that has been attacked, to prevent own nation being next in line
- **Milchemet reshut** (optional war)
  - acceptable only for good reasons
  - last resort
  - **Sanhedrin** (Jewish Council holding supreme religious authority) agrees (but no Sanhedrin for two millennia)
- Martyrs known as **Kiddush Hashem** (holy ones); they include those who died in **Shoah** (the Holocaust, i.e. the murder of over 6 million Jews by the Nazis) or who formed resistance in **Warsaw ghetto** (where Polish Jews were made to live by the Nazis)

Key words

Buddhism
skilful means
Christianity
forgiveness
peace
reconciliation
Hinduism
dharma yuddha
Gandhi
satyagraha
Islam
harb al-muqadis
lesser jihad
Judaism
Messianic era
Kiddush Hashem
milchemet mitzvah
milchemet reshut
Sanhedrin
Shoah
Warsaw ghetto
Sikhism
Ardas
dharma yudh
kirpan

Sikhism

- Sikhs support principle of ahimsa
- Guru Nanak pacifist: taught Sikhs to put up with hurt three times and said God would help if attacked a fourth time
- **Ardas** contains prayer for well-being of all humanity
- Later Gurus accepted war in defence of self or Sikh faith
- **Kirpan** (one of the Five Ks — the five symbols of Sikhism) originally used in self-defence but became symbol of religious freedom or being 'warrior' for faith
- **Dharma yudh** (Just War) part of Khalsa code and allowed
  - in self-defence
  - as last resort
  - where no desire for revenge
  - land/property seized in war to be returned at end of war
  - no looting
  - civilians not to be harmed
  - no use of mercenaries, as those fighting must believe in the cause
  - use of minimum force

 ## Case study

Mahatma Gandhi

TopFoto

- Born in India in 1869
- Trained as lawyer in London and then worked in South Africa
- Devout Hindu deeply influenced by principle of ahimsa
- Returned to India and became leader of struggle for independence from British rule
- Pacifist, so believed in non-violent resistance, e.g. protest marches
- Campaigned against caste system
- Tried to bring peace and trust between Hindus and Muslims and this resulted in his assassination in 1948

Case study

Dietrich Bonhoeffer

- Born in Germany in 1906
- Protestant Christian
- Studied theology and became a Lutheran pastor
- Co-founded the Confessing Church — which opposed Hitler and the Nazis
- Helped Jews escape from Germany
- Rejected earlier pacifist views because he believed that the evil of Nazism could be overcome only by violence
- Plotted overthrow of Hitler
- Arrested and eventually moved to Flossenburg concentration camp
- Hanged in April 1945
- Commemorated as a martyr by the Church of England

Statue of Dietrich Bonhoeffer who was commemorated as a martyr, Westminster Abbey

Case study

Cross of Nails centres

- In 1940 Coventry cathedral (along with much of Coventry) was destroyed by German bombs
- The Provost wrote the words 'Father forgive' on the sanctuary wall; two charred beams that had fallen in the shape of a cross were set up on the altar and three of the medieval nails were bound together in the shape of a cross
- Crosses of nails became a symbol of reconciliation and peace
- At the end of the war, crosses of nails were sent to German cities bombed by Allies
- There are now 160 Cross of Nails centres throughout the world, working for reconciliation and peace, e.g. in the Middle East (working with Jews and Arabs) and in South Africa (healing the terrible memories of apartheid)

Test yourself

1 Read through the following statements relating to the Second World War. Next to each, say which criterion of the Just War theory could be applied and then put a tick or cross, indicating whether you think it was fulfilled or not. The first has been done for you as an example

Statement	Criterion fulfilled	
The UK went to war with Germany because Hitler invaded Poland, with whom the UK had an alliance	*Just cause*	✓
The British government declared war on Germany		
Before declaring war, Britain had held talks with Hitler and made a treaty — but Hitler ignored it		
Britain had an army, a navy and an air force that were reasonably equipped		
Europe suffered terribly under Nazi rule. After the war, Eastern Europe was dominated by the Soviet Union and its repressive policies		
Thousands of civilians died in the bombing of Dresden by the RAF and allies		
The Americans dropped nuclear bombs on Hiroshima and Nagasaki		
When Germany surrendered, the British and Americans began to help German refugees		

2 Give three reasons why pacifists did not agree with the UK going to war against Germany in 1939.

3 Explain briefly two consequences of war.

Examination question

a **'Religious believers who fight in a war are betraying their faith.'**
   What do you think? Explain your opinion. *(3 marks)*

> **Exam tip**
>
> 3-mark evaluation questions do not require you to give two points of view.
> They want you to say what you think about the issue, giving reasons for the opinion
> you hold. You need to make sure that you read the stem (the quotation at the start
> of the question) very carefully so that your answer is focused and relevant.

b **Explain why many religious believers are pacifists.** *(6 marks)*

c **Explain why many Christians accept war in some situations.** *(6 marks)*

Religion and young people

Birth and initiation ceremonies

Many religions have ceremonies that celebrate the safe birth of children. They are a sign that life is precious and that children are a blessing. They are often occasions for giving thanks and for seeking God's blessing on the child as an assurance that he will support the child throughout his/her life. Sometimes they are occasions for parents to recognise their responsibilities in the spiritual as well as physical caring for the child.

Christianity

In font (contains water for baptism) near door — sign of entering Christian community

Parents and godparents promise to bring up baby as Christian

Signing with sign of cross — sign of being a 'soldier' for Christ

Water blessed and then poured three times over baby's forehead

'I baptise you in the name of the Father and of the Son and of the Holy Spirit. Amen'

Given candle as sign of light of Christ and for child to shine as light to the world

Christianity: infant baptism

Fotolia

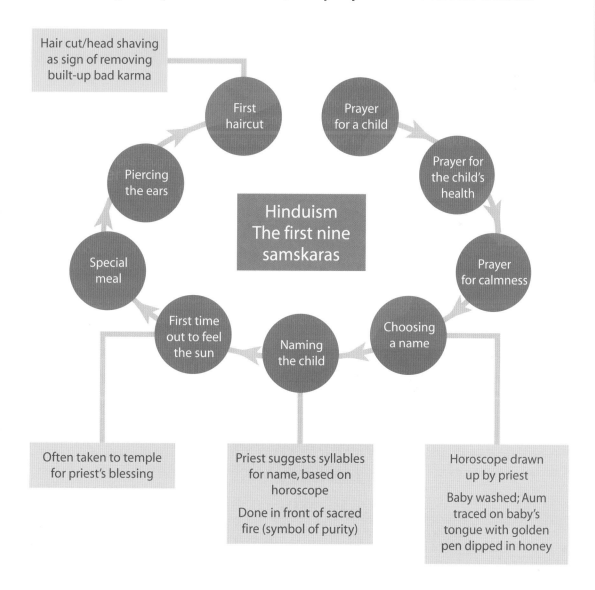

Most of the mainstream Christian denominations practise infant baptism. The child becomes a member of the Christian Church. There are two key parts to the rite: the use of water and the use of the Trinitarian formula (i.e. in the name of the Father and of the Son and of the Holy Spirit). The water symbolises the washing away of original sin (the inbuilt tendency to sin that is part of humanity) and a new start. The Baptist and Pentecostal churches do not practise infant baptism (see later in this chapter). Quakers and the Salvation Army do not have any form of baptism for infants or adults; they see no meaning in rituals.

Hinduism

A **samskara** is a rite of passage. There are 16 in total, each marking the individual's entry into a different state of life. Nowadays Hindus may not observe all of them. Namakarana, the 'naming ceremony', occurs when the baby is about 11 days old. The name given often reflects the religious aspirations for the child, or they may refer to the beauties of nature.

Hair cut/head shaving as sign of removing built-up bad karma

First haircut

Prayer for a child

Piercing the ears

Prayer for the child's health

Hinduism
The first nine samskaras

Special meal

Prayer for calmness

First time out to feel the sun

Naming the child

Choosing a name

Often taken to temple for priest's blessing

Priest suggests syllables for name, based on horoscope

Done in front of sacred fire (symbol of purity)

Horoscope drawn up by priest

Baby washed; Aum traced on baby's tongue with golden pen dipped in honey

Islam

The **adhan** is the call to prayer, and these are thought to be the first words a newborn baby should hear. The baby's first taste should be something sweet; hence the practice of **tahnik**. It follows the practice of Muhammad (pbuh). The shaving of the baby's head on the seventh day is a sign that the child is Allah's servant. **Aqiqah** (the sacrifice of sheep) also occurs on the seventh day, although in the UK the meat is ordered from the butcher. Circumcision (also often on the seventh day) reflects the story of Allah commanding Ibrahim to circumcise himself and Is'mail.

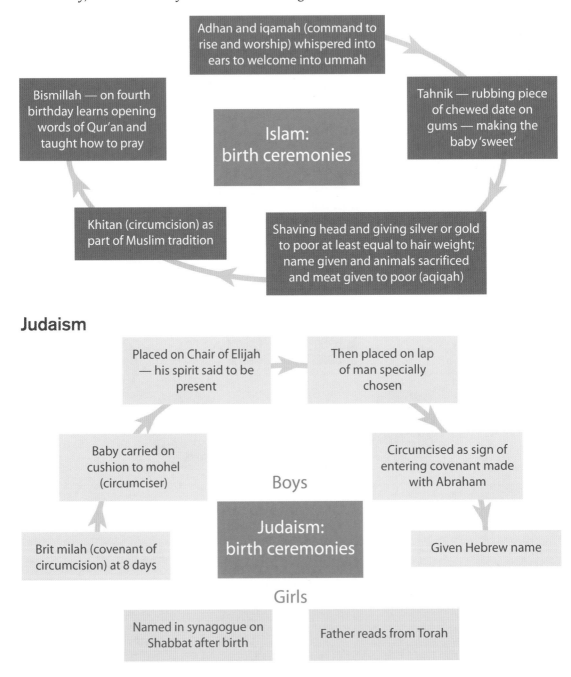

Adhan and iqamah (command to rise and worship) whispered into ears to welcome into ummah

Tahnik — rubbing piece of chewed date on gums — making the baby 'sweet'

Bismillah — on fourth birthday learns opening words of Qur'an and taught how to pray

Islam: birth ceremonies

Khitan (circumcision) as part of Muslim tradition

Shaving head and giving silver or gold to poor at least equal to hair weight; name given and animals sacrificed and meat given to poor (aqiqah)

Judaism

Placed on Chair of Elijah — his spirit said to be present

Then placed on lap of man specially chosen

Baby carried on cushion to mohel (circumciser)

Circumcised as sign of entering covenant made with Abraham

Boys

Brit milah (covenant of circumcision) at 8 days

Judaism: birth ceremonies

Given Hebrew name

Girls

Named in synagogue on Shabbat after birth

Father reads from Torah

According to the Torah (Genesis 17), circumcision was the seal of the covenant made by God with Abraham. Abraham was told to undergo the rite himself, and also to ensure that all his descendants were circumcised. Any who were not circumcised cut themselves off from the covenant relationship; they were not part of the Chosen People.

The importance of this ceremony is seen in the fact that it takes precedence over Shabbat. Only if it would endanger the baby's life may circumcision be postponed. Otherwise it always takes place at 8 days.

Sikhism

The ceremony associated with the birth of a child originated with Guru Angad. A Sikh took his baby son to the Guru and asked for his blessing. The Guru recited Japji, sprinkled holy water on the baby's head, face and eyes and then selected at random a letter from the Japji. This letter was used to name the child.

Key words	
Christianity	**Sikhism**
font	amrit
Hinduism	Guru Granth Sahib
samskara	kara
Islam	karah parshad
adhan	Kaur
aqiqah	romalla
bismillah	Singh
iqamah	
Khitan	
tahnik	
Judaism	
Brit milah	
mohel	

Baby brought before Guru Granth Sahib (Sikh sacred text) for naming

Granthi prepares amrit (sugared water) — stirs amrit with sword and says prayer

Ardas (general prayer) and special prayer for child said

Baby given kara (bracelet) — sign of Sikh community

Sikhism: birth ceremonies

Amrit dropped on lips — mother drinks rest

Karah parshad (food eaten in gurdwara) distributed — some put on baby's lips

Parents give romalla (cloth that covers Guru Granth Sahib) to gurdwara in thanks for child

Boy also named Singh (lion); girl also named Kaur (princess)

Guru Granth Sahib randomly opened — name given with first letter of first word

The home and upbringing

All religions think that parents and the wider family have an important part to play in the rearing of children.

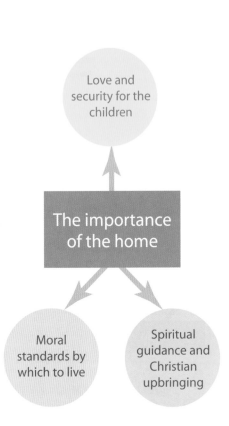

Love and security for the children

The importance of the home

Moral standards by which to live

Spiritual guidance and Christian upbringing

A Sikh family

Faith groups' provision for young people

Most religions make provision for young people as they are growing up. In the modern world, with all its pressures, it is easy for young people to drift away from their faith and to adopt the materialism and self-centred individualism that is prevalent in much of society. Religions may provide some of the following:

- groups that instruct young people in the essentials of their faith, e.g. classes attached to the mosque where young Muslims learn the Qur'an
- youth groups, e.g. **Boys' Brigade** and **Girls' Brigade**
- discussion groups
- holiday camps, e.g. **Spring Harvest**

Case study

Spring Harvest

- Spring Harvest is a Christian organisation catering for all age groups, but especially for young people
- It began in 1979 with just under 3,000 people attending the Spring Harvest camp. In 2008 there were 45,000 people
- At the camps there is a wide variety of religious activities: worship, guest speakers, dance, drama, Bible study etc.
- There are also leisure activities, e.g. swimming, football, go-karting
- It also owns a 4-star holiday park in France, where religious activities are provided for those who want them
- Spring Harvest publishes a number of magazines, Bible study aids, songbooks and CDs
- The Spring Harvest camps provide a distinctively Christian environment where young people can feel free to express, deepen and share their faith without fear of ridicule or hostility
- Spring Harvest also gives money each year to charity, e.g. supporting a project that cares for destitute children in Uganda

Case study

Taizé

- Christian community founded by Brother Roger in France
- After Brother Roger's death, leadership passed to Brother Alois
- Brothers take simple vows committing them to celibacy and community life
- Ecumenical community (i.e. the brothers come from different denominations)
- Thousands of young people from all over the world go each year to share in worship and Bible study/discussion groups
- Includes people of all faiths and no faith — very inclusive
- Five services each day
- Worship involves use of candles and singing devotional songs set to simple chants

Over 100,000 young people from around the world make pilgrimages to Taizé each year

Involvement in festivals

Young people are encouraged to participate in the festivals of their religions. Sometimes there are practices that young people can particularly enjoy, for example:

- making **Wesak** lanterns
- throwing coloured paint and water at **Holi**
- **Easter** egg rolling
- **Christingle** services

The Hindu festival Holi is celebrated by people throwing coloured powder and coloured water at each other

Membership and coming of age

Some, though not all, religions have specific ceremonies to mark commitment to the faith. Sometimes there is a set age, as in Judaism. In others there is not, though the time of adolescence is common.

Freedom of choice

But restricted by duty not to harm others

Young people: rights and responsibilities

Duty to obey rules of communities to which they belong, e.g. family, school, religious community

Relationships

Right to care from parents and support from religious community

Duty to honour parents and respect other people

Key words

Boys' Brigade
Christingle
Easter
Girls' Brigade
Holi
Spring Harvest
Wesak

Christianity

Baptist and Pentecostal churches (as well as individual churches in other denominations) practise **Believers' Baptism**. They believe that people should only be baptised when they are old enough to understand the commitment they are making and to make an informed choice. Believers' Baptism is also in the name of the **Trinity**. It takes the form of **total immersion** in a river or in a baptismal tank set into the floor of the church building. Before being baptised, the person makes a personal testimony of faith. The water symbolises death to the old way of life, with the person's sins washed away and resurrection to new life as a member of the Kingdom of God.

The Christian denominations that practise infant baptism usually have some ceremony at a later stage for teenagers or adults. At this ceremony they are able to make promises and the commitment for themselves that was made on their behalf at baptism. In some denominations, this takes the form of **Confirmation**. The ceremony varies slightly, but the meaning is the same. In the Anglican Church, the **bishop** lays his hands over the candidate's head, praying that the Holy Spirit might fill his/her life from now on. At Confirmation, the person becomes an adult member of the Church.

Young people make baptismal promises for themselves → Bishop lays hands on candidates' heads → Prayer for gift of Holy Spirit

Performed by bishop

Confirmation (for many denominations)

Now (if not already) communicant member of church

Christianity

May have dedication ceremony at birth

Believers' baptism (for Baptist and Pentecostal Christians)

Now communicant member of the church

Statement of repentance and of faith → Total immersion in baptismal pool/river → Baptism in the name of the Trinity

Hinduism

Upanayana means 'approaching God' and this samskara marks the start of the student stage of life. When the ceremony is complete, the child is ready to start studying, begin scriptures and to perform puja in the shrine at home. In modern times, it is a ceremony for boys, but in ancient times girls were included.

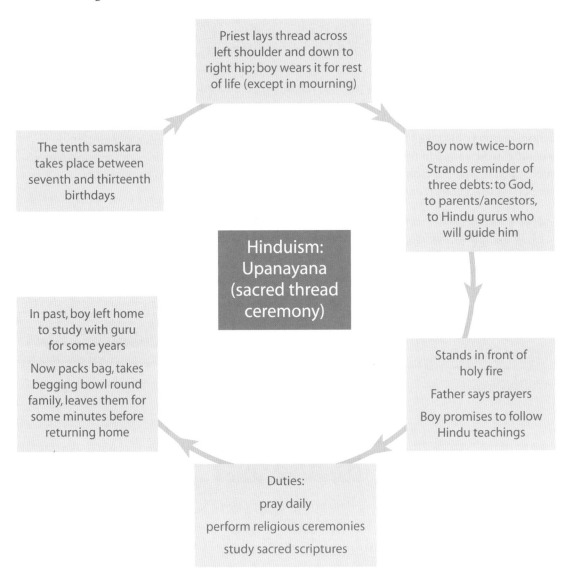

Priest lays thread across left shoulder and down to right hip; boy wears it for rest of life (except in mourning)

The tenth samskara takes place between seventh and thirteenth birthdays

Boy now twice-born

Strands reminder of three debts: to God, to parents/ancestors, to Hindu gurus who will guide him

Hinduism: Upanayana (sacred thread ceremony)

In past, boy left home to study with guru for some years

Now packs bag, takes begging bowl round family, leaves them for some minutes before returning home

Stands in front of holy fire

Father says prayers

Boy promises to follow Hindu teachings

Duties:

pray daily

perform religious ceremonies

study sacred scriptures

Judaism

For at least a year before the **Bar Mitzvah**, a Jewish boy will have attended synagogue classes, learning more about his faith, how to wear the **tallit** (prayer shawl) and **tefillin** (boxes containing Torah passges) and also learning how to read from the Torah. At the Bar Mitzvah, the boy becomes an adult in his faith, forming part of the minyan. He is now expected to obey all 613 Torah commandments.

The Bat Chayil/Bat Mitzvah ceremonies are relatively modern. Orthodox Jews believe that women have different (although equally important) roles. If they have any ceremony for girls it is much lower key than the Bar Mitzvah. Reform Jews on the other hand have an equivalent ceremony for girls.

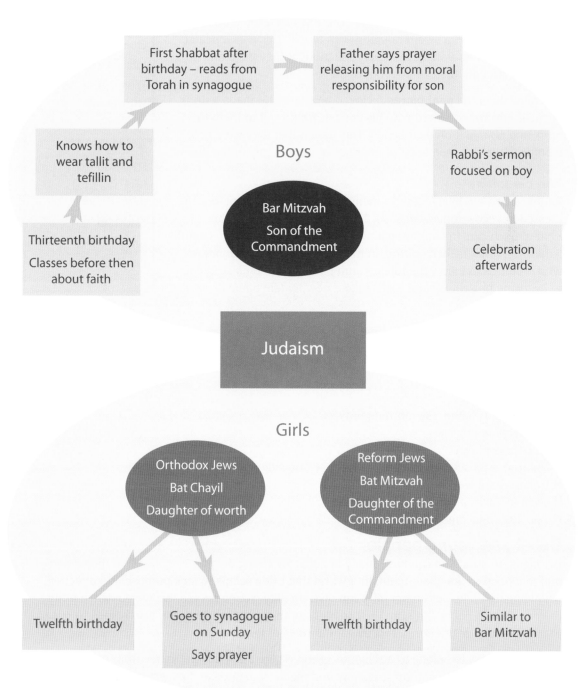

Sikhism

How the Amrit sanskar initiation rite began

Started by Guru Gobind Singh at festival of Baisakhi in 1699.
He asked for five volunteers to sacrifice their lives for their faith.

He took the first volunteer into a tent. There was a terrible thud and he reappeared with a sword dripping with blood. This was repeated with the other four volunteers. Everyone thought they were martyrs. Finally he brought the five men out of the tent, alive.

He called them the **panj piares** (beloved brothers). He made a drink of sugar and water, stirred with his dagger. He gave it to them to drink and poured it on their heads. This meant that they were now members (the first members) of the Khalsa (Community of the Pure).

The ceremony

Ritual carried out by five Khalsa members known as panj piares and dressed in yellow tunic with sash. They recite the duties of the Khalsa. Each stirs the amrit, reciting a passage from the Guru Granth Sahib. The amrit is then poured on the hair and eyes of the initiate, who promises to follow the rules. Karah parshad is then distributed to everyone present. Khalsa Sikhs take a new middle name or surname.

Key words

Christianity
Believers' baptism
bishop
Confirmation
total immersion
Trinity
Hinduism
Upanayana
Judaism
Bar Mitzvah
tallit
tefillin
Sikhism
Amrit sanskar
panj piare

Initiation can take place at any time from adolescence on. Both boys and girls can become members of the Khalsa. If they break the rules, they have to undergo Amrit sanskar again.

Duties of a Khalsa Sikh

- Wear the Five Ks
- Get up early, bathe, say morning prayers
- Say evening prayers
- Say Ardas prayer
- Not to use tobacco/intoxicants or have sex outside marriage
- Honest, hard work to provide for family
- Treat all Sikhs as brothers and sisters
- Give 10% of income to poor

Belief and young people

Belonging to a religion can have many benefits for young people. They feel that they belong and that people care about them. In a world that often seems to lack purpose and direction, belonging to a religious community can give stability. Young people receive guidance from their religious leaders and from the teachings of their religion. They are also helped to reject the temptations of drugs etc. because of the rules of their religion.

But it is not easy to belong to a religious group. There are many pressures from outside to reject religion and to conform to society and media standards and expectations.

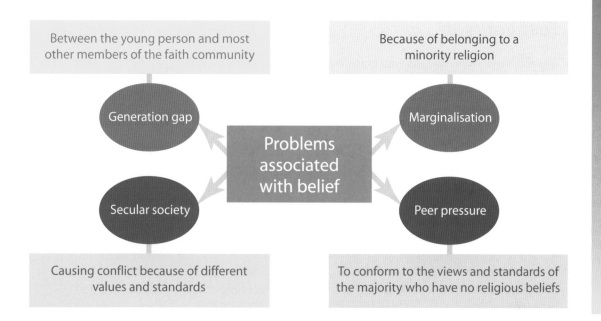

Religion in schools

By law, all schools are expected to hold regular assemblies and to provide religious studies right through secondary school. Religious studies provides young people with a unique opportunity to explore the beliefs and practices of different religious traditions and to discuss a wide variety of philosophical and moral issues. Some schools are faith schools. Pupils who attend them follow the same curriculum as in other schools but there is a strong emphasis on a particular faith and a particular set of values:

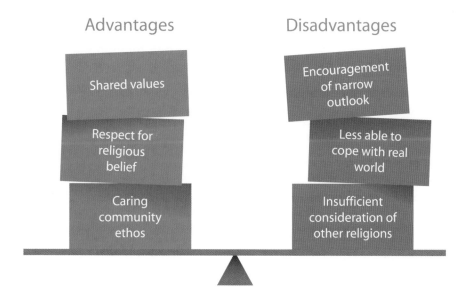

Test yourself

Case study

Youth SVP

- SVP stands for St Vincent de Paul Society
- The Youth SVP was set up in Paris by some university students
- It is found all over the world and since the start of this century there have been over 10,000 members in England and Wales
- It is the largest Roman Catholic youth organisation in England and Wales
- Many SVP groups are based in schools
- They seek to help those who are disadvantaged in some way, e.g. helping at swimming clubs for disabled people, working at drop-in centres for elderly and lonely people, helping at charity shops, listening to pupils read, teaching computer skills to retired people
- Each year there is a camp where members of Youth SVP from many different backgrounds meet one another and enjoy all kinds of activities

1 Why do you think so many Roman Catholic young people join the Youth SVP?

2 Think about the area you live in and suggest two ways in which the Youth SVP might help the community.

3 Why do you think many young people might want to go to the Youth SVP camp rather than on a family holiday to Spain?

Examination question

a **Describe what happens at a birth ceremony in one religion that you have studied.** *(4 marks)*

b **Explain the importance of the birth ceremony you have described.** *(4 marks)*

c **'Faith schools just encourage young people to be prejudiced.'**

Do you agree? Give reasons for your answer, showing that you have thought about more than one point of view. Refer to religious arguments in your answer. *(6 marks)*

Exam tip

In answering 6-mark evaluation questions, make sure that you give more than one viewpoint. A one-sided answer can be awarded no more than 4 marks. If all your evaluation responses are one-sided, your final exam grade might well be affected.

Key word index